Vince Flynn, Brad Thor, Tom Clancy, James Patterson, David Baldacci, John Grisham, Brad Meltzer, Daniel Silva, Don DeLillo

If you like these TV series –
House of Cards, Scandal, West Wing, The Good Wife,

Madam Secretary, Designated Survivor

You'll love the **unputdownable** series about
Jack Houston St. Clair, with political intrigue, romance,
and loads of action and suspense.

Besides writing travel books, I've written political thrillers
for many years that have delighted hundreds of thousands
of readers. I want to introduce you to my work!
Send me an email and I'll send you a link where you can
download the first 3 books in my bestselling series,
absolutely FREE.

Mention **this book** when you email me.

andrewdelaplaine@mac.com

NEW ORLEANS
2020

The Food Enthusiast's
Complete Restaurant Guide

Andrew Delaplaine

Andrew Delaplaine is the Food Enthusiast.
When he's not playing tennis,
he dines anonymously
at the Publisher's expense.

Gramercy Park Press
New York London Paris
Cover Photo by Rosie Kerr on Unsplash
Copyright © by Gramercy Park Press - All rights
reserved.

DID YOU FIND AN INTERESTING PLACE?

If you discover a place you think I should check out
on my next visit, drop me a line, will you? I'll
mention your name if I end up listing it.
andrewdelaplaine@mac.com

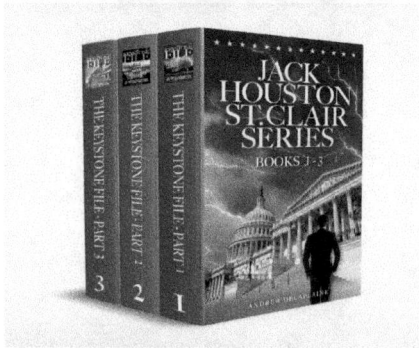

WANT 3 *FREE* THRILLERS?

Why, of course you do!

If you like these writers--

The Food Enthusiast's
Complete Restaurant Guide

Table of Contents

Introduction

In all my years of travel, I've always maintained that there are only a handful of cities in the U.S. that are thoroughly unique.

Of course, every place is unique *technically,* but what I mean by that is you'd be hard pressed to tell me the difference between Florence, S.C., and Darlington, S.C., if you were to drive through them. Or for that matter Sumter, S.C. Though they're different from each other, they're not *substantially* different. They're Podunk little towns in South Carolina that have nothing to distinguish them except the road that luckily leads you out of them to some more interesting place. (I know. I lived in a town like that when I was a kid. Never again.)

New Orleans is not a town you can say that about.

With its rich cultural diversity (going back to the 1600s) that mixes in the French, the African, the Creole, the Spanish—and a lot of other influences— New Orleans is a fragrant stew of Life.

This is the birthplace of Jazz, which dates back to around 1910. I've always found it puzzling why Jazz is so unknown to younger audiences. It's such an American institution, but it doesn't seem to have found its place among the younger audiences today.

Since Katrina, there have been lots of great new restaurants that have opened, giving the city a food scene that rivals in richness what famous Southern chefs are doing in places like Charleston and Savannah.

And while you're sure to head straight to the French Quarter if this is your first visit, be sure to explore the Garden District if just to see the fabulous houses. You'll wish you lived in one of them.

Next to the French Quarter is the Central Business District (CBD) where the Superdome is located along with lots of museums.

Crime has gone up since Katrina, so you want to beware of certain areas. Ask your hotel or host if you have any questions. Most tourist areas are safe, however. Beware of hustles and pickpockets.

Also, there's a local saying, "Nothing good happens in the Quarter after midnight," and it's true. The bouncers and other security personnel in the clubs can be really nasty when dealing with drunks, and many have been sent to the hospital. Do not argue with them. You will not win.

Even with all my warnings, don't let me give you the impression you should think twice about coming here. You'd be *crazy* not to visit New Orleans if you have the chance. Arriving here always sends your senses into overdrive, into a fever pitch, whether it's your first time here or your tenth or thirtieth.

The uncomfortable muggy summer is the season that for me evokes the true sense of New Orleans. There's something about the town that makes you feel "air conditioning" is wrong. (Although it's a blessed relief to have it—I'm just talking metaphorically.) You wonder how people ever lived in the vortex of sweat and the smell of rotting tropical plants.

Those smells.

The humidity.

The jasmine.

The wrought iron grilles adorning the houses.

The smell of fried seafood.

The different dialects.

The St. Charles Avenue streetcar, still un-air-conditioned after all these years with its open windows and wooden benches.

The cemeteries that are more eerie than any others.

The music, the music, the music.

The rich Uptown lawyers taking their time over 4-hour lunches at Galatoire's while they swill down French burgundy and eat oysters Rockefeller.

The serenity of the Garden District.

The craziness of the Quarter.

It's all just too much. And all too wonderful.

* * *

How to say it: Don't use "Nawlins." The best way for an out-of-towner to say it is: *noo-OHR-luhnz*.

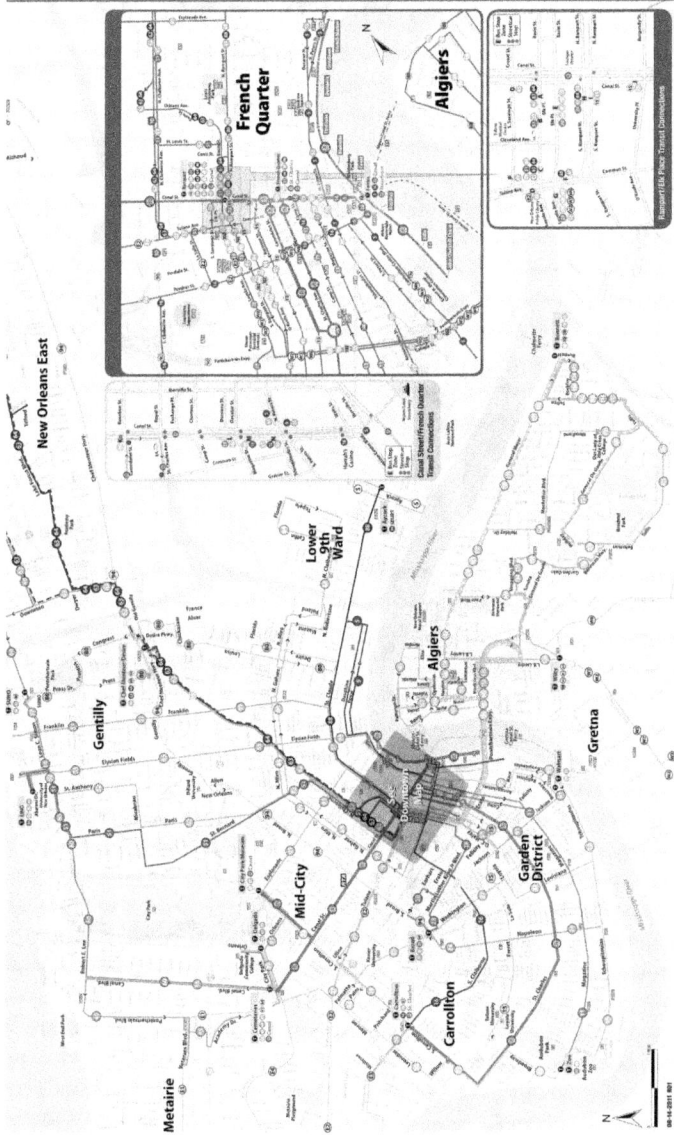

13

The A to Z Listings

Ridiculously Extravagant
Sensible Alternatives
Quality Bargain Spots

ACME OYSTER HOUSE
724 Iberville St, New Orleans, 504-522-5973
www.acmeoyster.com

CUISINE: Seafood
DRINKS: Full Bar
SERVING: Lunch, Dinner
PRICE RANGE: $$
NEIGHBORHOOD: French Quarter
For more than 100 years this New Orleans eatery has been offering up delicious seafood dishes. Menu favorites include the fresh, hand-shucked oysters and Seafood Gumbo. There's often a wait for tables but it's worth it just to see the shuckers do their thing. On a stage this would be called performance art.

AGLIO
611 O'Keefe Ave, New Orleans, 504-827-1090
www.aglionola.com
CUISINE: Sandwiches / Italian
DRINKS: Full Bar
SERVING: Lunch, Dinner
PRICE RANGE: $$
NEIGHBORHOOD: Warehouse District

Neighborhood deli specializing in fresh sandwiches, soups, and salads. Excellent fig cookies made with semisweet shortbread. Vegetarian and gluten-free options. Bar offers handcrafted cocktails and a nice variety of wines.

ANCORA PIZZERIA
4508 Freret St, New Orleans, 504-324-1636
www.ancorapizza.com
CUISINE: Pizza
DRINKS: Full Bar
SERVING: Dinner
PRICE RANGE: $$
NEIGHBORHOOD: Uptown/Freret
This pizzeria serves authentic Neapolitan pizzas and house-made salumi. The *arancini* (Sicilian fried rice balls coated with breadcrumbs) is wildly good. They also offer a great selection of Italian wines and hand-crafted cocktails. Closed Sundays.

ARNAUD'S

813 Bienville Ave, New Orleans, 504-523-5433
www.arnaudsrestaurant.com
CUISINE: Cajun/Creole
DRINKS: Full Bar
SERVING: Dinner
PRICE RANGE: $$$
NEIGHBORHOOD: French Quarter
Located just off Bourbon Street, this legendary eatery
is the picture image of what you think of when you
think of New Orleans, with its tile floor and the
wrought iron porches. They serve classic Creole
cuisine in an elegant atmosphere. The main dining
room offers the perfect setting for romantic dinner
and guests can enjoy live Dixieland Jazz in the **Jazz
Bistro**. Menu favorites include: Rainbow Trout with
Creole Sauce and Arnaud's Crab Cakes.

ATCHAFALAYA
901 Louisiana Ave, New Orleans, 504-891-9626

www.atchafalayarestaurant.com
CUISINE: Cajun/Creole
DRINKS: Full Bar
SERVING: Dinner nightly, Lunch daily except Tues & Wed
PRICE RANGE: $$
NEIGHBORHOOD: East Riverside
Some come for the build your own Bloody Mary bar. However, it's the food that keeps them coming back. Menu favorites include: Fried Chicken N Biscuits, eggs "treme" (they use crawfish in this dish) and Shrimp & Grits. Save room for the Blue Cheese Flan made with reduced balsamic and pumpkin seed brittle.

AUGUST
301 Tchoupitoulas St, New Orleans, 504-299-9777
www.restaurantaugust.com
CUISINE: French / Creole
DRINKS: Full Bar
SERVING: Dinner nightly; Lunch on Friday

PRICE RANGE: $$$$
NEIGHBORHOOD: Central Business District
Chef John Besh offers a creative menu of French cuisine in a beautifully decorated 19th century space. Striking chandeliers hang from high ceilings in this charming eatery. Brick walls are buttressed by ornate columns, giving the place an air of authority. Menu favorites include: Smoke swordfish cru and Crispy branzino with royal red shrimp. Or one of my favorites, the chili-enhanced soft shell crab. Reservations recommended.

BAKERY BAR
1179 Annunciation St, New Orleans, 504-513-8664
www.bakery.bar
CUISINE: Desserts
DRINKS: Full Bar
SERVING: Lunch, Dinner
PRICE RANGE: $$
NEIGHBORHOOD: Lower Garden District
Unique neighborhood spot with a bakery inspired menu and craft cocktails. Everything from cookies to cakes and cheese and charcuterie boards. There's a local favorite—the 7-layer "doberge" cake, with multiple flavors like cinnamon and chocolate. Board gamers paradise.

BEVI SEAFOOD CO
236 Carrollton Ave, New Orleans, 504-488-7503
www.beviseafoodco.com
CUISINE: Seafood/Sandwiches
DRINKS: Full bar

SERVING: Lunch & Dinner – Tues – Sat; Lunch
only Sun & Mon
PRICE RANGE: $$
NEIGHBORHOOD: Mid-City
Market and restaurant in simple surroundings. Menu
offers fresh fish, oysters and excellent po'boys. Try
their combo – high po-boy and cup of soup. Or go for
the Peacemaker, a big po'boy that includes Louisiana
fried shrimp, roast beef & Swiss cheese.

THE BON TON CAFÉ
401 Magazine St, New Orleans, 504-524-3386
www.thebontoncafe.com
CUISINE: Cajun / Creole
DRINKS: Full Bar
SERVING: Lunch & Dinner; closed Sat & Sun
PRICE RANGE: $$$
NEIGHBORHOOD: Central Business District
Open since 1953, this quaint eatery offers a menu of
classic Cajun dishes. Favorites include the Turtle
soup, the shrimp and crab okra gumbo and the
Crawfish Jambalaya. Get out your Crystal hot sauce.
Save room for their delicious Bread pudding.

BRIGTSEN'S
723 Dante St, New Orleans, 504-861-7610
www.brigtsens.com
CUISINE: Cajun/Creole, Southern
DRINKS: Full Bar
SERVING: Lunch, Dinner
PRICE RANGE: $$$
NEIGHBORHOOD: Uptown

Located in a homey Victorian cottage, Brigtsen's serves a menu of classic South Louisiana cuisine with dishes like Pan-Roasted Pork Chop and BBQ Seasoned Redfish with Chipotle Grits Cake. Save room for one of their delicious desserts like their incredible Pecan Pie or the Lemon Ice Box Creme Brulee. This is an elegant dining experience you won't forget.

BORGNE
601 Loyola Ave, New Orleans, 504-613-3860
www.borgnerestaurant.com
CUISINE: Seafood/American/Southern
DRINKS: Full Bar
SERVING: Lunch, Dinner
PRICE RANGE: $$$
NEIGHBORHOOD: Central Business District
This is a favorite destination for local seafood and Southern dishes. It's a very simple room, big and open and airy, and sends off the same vibe you get at the fish camps that you run across when traveling along the waterways. Menu favorites include: Louisiana White Shrimp Risotto, a spicy shrimp rémoulade, Stuffed Flounder and Sheepshead Fish in a Bag. The desserts are also worth trying like the Lime Ice Box Parfait and the Chocolate Hazelnut Puddin.

BOUCHERIE
8115 Jeannette St, New Orleans, 504-862-5514
www.boucherie-nola.com
CUISINE: Barbeque/Southern
DRINKS: Full Bar
SERVING: Lunch, Dinner
PRICE RANGE: $$
NEIGHBORHOOD: Uptown
One would never think that this Southern-flavored
bistro began its life as a food truck. The menu is quite
inventive with dishes like Boudin balls and Krispy
Kreme bread pudding. Menu favorites include:
Blackened shrimp with grit toast and Wagyu Beef
Brisket.

BOULIGNY TAVERN
3641 Magazine St, New Orleans, 504-891-1810
www.boulignytavern.com

CUISINE: Tapas/Small Plates
DRINKS: Full Bar
SERVING: Dinner, Late night
PRICE RANGE: $$
NEIGHBORHOOD: East Riverside

This relaxed eatery is basically a gastropub that offers small-plate dining. Menu favorites include croquettes with chorizo and comte, gouda beignets and meatball flatbread. They also offer an impressive list of selected wines and a well-crafted cocktail menu with exotic drink specialties like the Sage Julep. Closed Sundays.

BOURBON HOUSE

144 Bourbon St, New Orleans, 504-522-0111
www.bourbonhouse.com
CUISINE: Cajun/Creole
DRINKS: Full Bar
SERVING: Lunch, Dinner
PRICE RANGE: $$$
NEIGHBORHOOD: French Quarter

Chef Dickie Brennan is well known in New Orleans and offers a menu of great Cajun/Creole cuisine. Menu favorites include: New Orleans Style BBQ Shrimp and Redfish on the Half Shell, though I'm especially fond of the oysters with caviar and Parmesan. This is truly a fine dining experience. And for the bourbon, this place offers an impressive selection of small batch and single barrel bourbons. If you're a bourbon fan, you must try the Frozen Bourbon Milk Punch—it's basically a milkshake, but one you won't soon forget.

BROUSSARD'S

819 Conti St, New Orleans, 504-581-3866
www.broussards.com
CUISINE: Seafood, French, and Cajun/Creole
DRINKS: Full Bar
SERVING: Lunch, Dinner
PRICE RANGE: $$$
NEIGHBORHOOD: French Quarter
A New Orleans fixture for nearly a century,
Broussard's offers a menu that mixes French and
Creole influences. Here you'll get a dining experience
that you won't forget. Menu favorites include: Oven
Baked Dover Sole and Gulf Shrimp Lean Lafitte.
Desserts are tasty too with selections like Crepes
Broussard and the Bananas Foster.

CAFÉ SBISA

1011 Decatur St, New Orleans, 504-522-5565
www.cafesbisanola.com

CUISINE: Southern/Seafood
DRINKS: Full Bar
SERVING: Dinner, Lunch on Sun; Closed Mon &
Tues
PRICE RANGE: $$
NEIGHBORHOOD: French Quarter
Ornately decorated venue offering classic (and
expertly prepared) French-Creole cuisine since 1899.
They had lots of damage during Hurricane Katrina,
but recovered eventually. Check out the daily
gumbos—they're great whatever the day happens to
be. Favorites: Turtle soup and Louisiana Blue Crab
Cakes. Nice wine selection.

CANE & TABLE
1113 Decatur St, New Orleans, 504-581-1112
www.caneandtablenola.com
CUISINE: Caribbean
DRINKS: Full Bar
SERVING: Dinner
PRICE RANGE: $$
NEIGHBORHOOD: French Quarter
This eatery has an old-world ambience (what you
might imagine a Colonial-era pub or inn might feel
like) with a menu of primarily small plates. Favorites
include their delicious ribs soaked in El Dorado rum,
braised in ginger, garlic, peppers. Ther ribs are then
battered and deep-fried, which gives you a crispy
shell surrounding the succulent ribs. The craft
cocktails emphasize good aged rums and employ
house-made syrups to finish them off perfectly.

CASAMENTO'S
4330 Magazine St, New Orleans, 504-895-9761
www.casamentosrestaurant.com
CUISINE: Seafood
DRINKS: Full Bar
SERVING: Lunch daily, Dinner Thurs. – Sat; closed
Sun
PRICE RANGE: $$
NEIGHBORHOOD: East Riverside
Cut little seafood eatery, open since 1919, that's a
little off the beaten path but worth the search. Cash-
only spot serves fresh oysters & other seafood in a
compact, mosaic-tiled space.

COCHON BUTCHER
930 Tchoupitoulas St, New Orleans, 504-588-7675
www.cochonbutcher.com
CUISINE: Sandwiches
DRINKS: Full Bar
SERVING: Lunch, Dinner
PRICE RANGE: $$
NEIGHBORHOOD: Central Business District /
Warehouse District
No-frills butcher shop offering a great selection of
sandwiches, with an emphasis on the muffuletta,
which they serve hot unless you order it cold. The
chef has a special oven to heat them, using a
combination of steam and heat that melts the cheese
to highlight the flavors of the meat. Try the Le Pig
Mac – their version of the Big Mac and the Duck
Pastrami Slider. Butcher counter with selection of
meats. Le Pig Mac, the mac and cheese and blueberry
cheesecake.Menu favorites include: Buckboard

Bacon Melt, Rabbit & Dumplings and Roasted
Turkey with Arugula, Tomato and Fontina.
The butcher shop offers in-house made meats,
terrines, sausages, and fresh cut meats. Great place
for catering needs. No reservations.

COMMANDER'S PALACE
1403 Washington Ave, New Orleans, 504-899-8221
www.commanderspalace.com
CUISINE: Cajun/Creole
DRINKS: Full Bar
SERVING: Lunch, Dinner
PRICE RANGE: $$$$
NEIGHBORHOOD: Garden District
This place gets as much hype as a tourist trap but
there's a difference: this is the "Real Thing." In a
classic Victorian setting, this eatery offers a menu
that combines modern New Orleans cooking with

Haute Creole. This is the place decades ago where French Creole and Cajun were first blended with nouvelle cuisine. There have been many copycats, and many of them are very good, but this place still sets a very high bar. Though the place can be quite expensive, one tip followed frequently by locals is to head here for lunch on weekdays when it's always very cheap. (The used to sell 25-cent martinis, limit of 3, and they might still do that.) Menu favorites include: Pecan Crusted Gulf Fish, Absinthe Poached Oysters, Turtle Soup (spiked with sherry) and Cast Iron Seared Foie Gras. You can't leave without trying the bread pudding soufflé. The bar offers a creative cocktail menu with selections like the Vieux Carre Cocktail. The white-glove service is impeccable.

THE COMPANY BURGER
4600 Freret St, New Orleans, 504-267-0320
www.thecompanyburger.com
CUISINE: Burgers/Fast Food
DRINKS: Full Bar
SERVING: Lunch, Dinner

PRICE RANGE: $$
NEIGHBORHOOD: Uptown
As the name suggests, this place specializes in
burgers of the thin patty type cooked on a griddle.
They are really juicy and tasty. They have a selection
of great burgers served with homemade condiments.
There's also the "Curewich," nicknamed for the
nearby bar **CURE**, because so many of the staff order
it: it's a grilled cheese with bacon and egg. The
owner's mother bakes the delicious desserts.

COMPERE LAPIN
535 Tchoupitoulas St, New Orleans, 504-599-2119
www.comperelapin.com
CUISINE: American/Caribbean
DRINKS: Full Bar
SERVING: Lunch & Dinner
PRICE RANGE: $$$
NEIGHBORHOOD: Warehouse District

Located in The Old No. 77 Hotel & Chandlery, Chef/Owner Nina Compton's menu features a combination of Caribbean, French, and Italian influences. (She's from St. Lucia and her grandmother was British.) Menu favorites include: Curried Goat and Broiled Shrimp.

THE COUNTRY CLUB
634 Louisa St, New Orleans, 504-945-0742
www.thecountryclubneworleans.com
CUISINE: American/Southern
DRINKS: Full Bar
SERVING: Lunch, Dinner
PRICE RANGE: $$
NEIGHBORHOOD: Bywater
This Country Club offers a party atmosphere with a clothing optional pool and hot tub but some people go just for the delicious food. Chef Maryjane Rosas offers a menu with a variety of treats from chicken and waffles to BBQ delicacies. Menu favorites include: Honey Lamb Roast and Seared Trout with Roasted Kohlrabi. This is also a popular Brunch destination.

COURT OF TWO SISTERS
613 Royal St, New Orleans, 504-522-7261
www.courtoftwosisters.com
CUISINE: American/Southern
DRINKS: Full Bar
SERVING: Breakfast, Lunch, Dinner
PRICE RANGE: $$$
NEIGHBORHOOD: French Quarter
This venerable establishment dates back to 1832. What you want to experience here is the courtyard

with its overflowing vines of wisteria creating a luscious canopy overhead. Crawfish omelets, Cajun past and Creole jambalaya are big dishes here. Their brunch consistently wins awards. A jazz band is usually working the crowd.

DAT DOG
5030 Rue Freret St, 504-899-6883
3336 Magazine St (Uptown), 504-324-2226
601 Frenchmen St (The Marigny), 504-309-3362
www.datdognola.com
CUISINE: Fast Food
DRINKS: Full Bar
SERVING: Lunch & Dinner
PRICE RANGE: $

Famous for their gourmet hot dogs (some made with crawfish and alligator) served with whatever you want on them on sourdough rolls. Toppings include guacamole, Andouille sauce, hummus, etc. Very creative hot dog menu.

THE DELACHAISE
3442 St. Charles Ave, New Orleans, 504-895-0858
www.thedelachaise.com
CUISINE: American
DRINKS: Full Bar
SERVING: Dinner
PRICE RANGE: $$
NEIGHBORHOOD: Central City/Uptown
This is a popular watering hole for preppies and hipsters who love the impressive selection of wine and beer. The menu includes favorites like Flank Steak Bruschetta and Moules et Frites. The food is

really just a step up from bar fare but it's creative and tasty.

DIMARTINO'S
700 S. Tyler, Covington, 985-276-6460
www.dimartinos.com
CUISINE: Muffulettas
DRINKS: No Booze
SERVING: Lunch & Dinner
PRICE RANGE: $$
NEIGHBORHOOD: Covington
Popular eatery with counter-serve. Menu of muffulettas, po'boys, burgers, and Italian entrees. Favorites: their signature dish - DiMartino's Famous New Orleans Muffuletta and Grilled Chicken Italian Salad. Eat in or to go.

DOMENICA
123 Baronne St, New Orleans, 504-648-6020
www.domenicarestaurant.com
CUISINE: Italian/Tapas
DRINKS: Full Bar
SERVING: Lunch, Dinner
PRICE RANGE: $$
NEIGHBORHOOD: Central Business District
Located inside the Roosevelt Hotel, this John Besh restaurant offers delicious Italian fare. Menu favorites include: Roasted Carrot pizza and Rigatoni. Save room for the Gianduja Budino, a delicious dessert. You'll also find a menu of custom-brewed beers and Italian wines.

DOMILISE'S PO'BOY & BAR

5240 Annunciation St, New Orleans, 504-899-9126
www.domilisespoboys.com
CUISINE: Barbeque/Seafood
DRINKS: Beer & Wine Only
SERVING: Lunch & Dinner; closed Sun
PRICE RANGE: $$$
NEIGHBORHOOD: West Riverside; Uptown
Local counter-serve eatery offering up giant po' boys
and beers makes this one of the highlights of your
visit. Don't let the fact that the place needs a paint job
deter you. When you get a look at the tiny kitchen
here, you'll wonder how these guys turn out the
wonderful food that they do in such quantities. While
you can order the usual suspects when it comes to
po'boys (fried oyster, fried shrimp and roast beef), I
always opt for one of their other po'boys, like the
cheeseburger po'boy or the smoked hot sausage.
Their condiments (hot sauces, mustards, etc.) are
better than average, far better.

DONG PHUONG BAKERY & RESTAURANT

14207 Chef Menteur Hwy, New Orleans, 504-254-
0214
http://dpbakeshop.com
CUISINE: Vietnamese/Chinese
DRINKS: No Booze
SERVING: Lunch, Dinner
PRICE RANGE: $
NEIGHBORHOOD: East New Orleans
There are two sides to this place, the bakery side and
the restaurant side. An amazing selection of baked
goods and pastries on that side, while over in the

restaurant, expect a large variety of Vietnamese dishes. There's quite a large Vietnamese population in NOLA, so I've listed some of the best spots. This one is good for take-out. The bakery provides breads to many local restaurants so you know it's good.

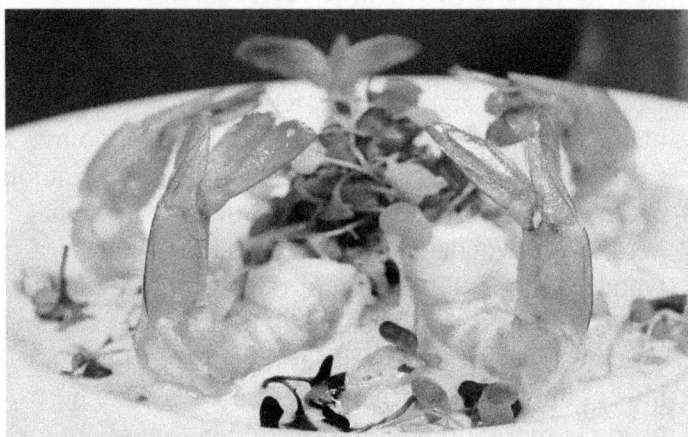

DRAGO'S SEAFOOD RESTAURANT
2 Poydras St, New Orleans, 504-584-3911
www.dragosrestaurant.com
CUISINE: Seafood
DRINKS: Full Bar
SERVING: Lunch, Dinner
PRICE RANGE: $$
NEIGHBORHOOD: Central Business District
This is a classic New Orleans seafood eatery with an impressive menu. Menu favorites include: Lobster and Shrimp & Grits. Many favor their classic oysters, and this would be a good place to savor a Crescent City specialty, **Charbroiled Oysters**, made with garlic, herbs and butter, topped with flaky parmesan and Romano cheese. The last time I was here, I easily

consumed 2 dozen of these mouthwatering delicacies.
There's also a gluten-free menu.

DTB
8201 Oak St, New Orleans, 504-518-6889
www.dtbnola.com
CUISINE: Cajun/Seafood
DRINKS: Full Bar
SERVING: Dinner, Lunch Fri - Sun
PRICE RANGE: $$
NEIGHBORHOOD: Leonidas
Chic eatery (located in a cottage near the Ace Hotel
dating back to 1832) offering a menu of modern
Cajun fare that evokes the Creole coastline. (DTB
means "down the bayou.") Favorites: Stuffed banana
beignets, Rice bowls with shrimp & crab, and
Mushroom Boudin Balls. Creative cocktails and nice
wine list.

EAT
900 Dumaine St, New Orleans, 504-522-7222
www.eatnola.com
CUISINE: Creole/Cajun/Soul Food
DRINKS: No Booze
SERVING: Lunch & Dinner, weekend Brunch;
closed Mon
PRICE RANGE: $$
NEIGHBORHOOD: French Quarter
This gay-operated hipster hangout is a cut above most
French Quarter spots. They have updated takes on
classic New Orleans dishes like BBQ shrimp,
crawfish & red beans, smoked salmon atop deviled

eggs. It's all in a charming brick and pale-blue dining room.

ELIZABETH'S
601 Gallier St, New Orleans, 504-944-9272
www.elizabethsrestaurantnola.com
CUISINE: Southern
DRINKS: Full Bar
SERVING: Breakfast, Lunch & Dinner; No Dinner on Sun
PRICE RANGE: $$
NEIGHBORHOOD: Bywater
This busy spot offers down-home country classics and great po' boys. Dishes are huge. Great spot for breakfast. (Order the French toast stuffed with bananas Foster, out of this world.)

EMERIL'S DELMONICO
1300 St Charles Ave, New Orleans, 504-525-4937

www.emerilsrestaurants.com
CUISINE: Cajun/Creole
DRINKS: Full Bar
SERVING: Dinner
PRICE RANGE: $$$
NEIGHBORHOOD: Mid-City; Lower Garden District

Located on the St. Charles Avenue streetcar line, this legendary eatery offers an impressive menu of Cajun and Creole dishes. Emeril pays special attention to his flagship restaurant and the menu changes 3 or 4 times a year, keeping it fresh and alive. Menu favorites include: Moulard Duck Breast and Beef & Pork Terrine. His version of the local favorite, "Dirty Rice," includes crispy pork cheek and scallions. Save room for dessert and order the Bananas Foster for two that's prepared at your table, you won't be disappointed. His version of the local favorite, "Dirty Rice," includes crispy pork cheek and scallions. Save room for dessert and order the Bananas Foster for two that's prepared at your table, you won't be disappointed.

FETE AU FETE
St Roch Market
2381 St Claude Ave, New Orleans, 504-475-7979
www.feteaufete.com
CUISINE: Food Trucks, Cajun/Creole, Southern
DRINKS: No Booze
SERVING: Breakfast, Lunch, & Dinner
PRICE RANGE: $$
NEIGHBORHOOD: St. Roch

Here in a stall in the St Roch Market (a restored food hall in a building that goes back to 1875) you'll find a true Southern food truck experience offering creative dishes like Trash Grits, Red Beans & rice with andouille sausage, Gumbo ya-ya, and Crawfish poutine. But the chef's muffuletta is exceptional. He serves his by the quarter rather than the full sandwich, and his is different because he presses them, squeezing the bread flat and making it crispy, more like a Cuban sandwich. The effect is quite good—he says the pressing makes a good sandwich into an outstanding one by rendering the fat out of the meat and softening up the olive salad. Well worth seeking out this little spot.

GALATOIRE'S
209 Bourbon St, New Orleans, 504-525-2021
www.galatoires.com

CUISINE: French
DRINKS: Full Bar
SERVING: Lunch, Dinner
PRICE RANGE: $$$
NEIGHBORHOOD: French Quarter
This French eatery specializes in old-fashioned
Creole cuisine. Menu favorites include: Duck Crepes
and Trout Almandine Meuniere. It's a two-level
restaurant with some of the upstairs rooms
overlooking Bourbon Street. This place is busy but no
reservations are accepted.

GAUTREAU'S
1728 Soniat St, New Orleans, 504-899-7397
www.gautreausrestaurant.com/
CUISINE: American (New) / French
DRINKS: Full Bar
SERVING: Dinner; closed Sun
PRICE RANGE: $$$
NEIGHBORHOOD: Uptown

A little secluded eatery that offers a menu of New American-French cuisine. Favorites include: Duck confit and Halibut, pork cheek with Korean chili glaze. Try their banana split – it's a winner.

GREEN GODDESS
307 Exchange Pl, New Orleans, 504-301-3347
www.greengoddessrestaurant.com
CUISINE: American/Vegetarian
DRINKS: Full Bar
SERVING: Lunch, Dinner
PRICE RANGE: $$
NEIGHBORHOOD: French Quarter
Here you'll find traditional New Orleans fare that has been influence by a variety of cultures. Menu dishes include French, Thai, Cajun and Soul. Menu also includes vegetarian and vegan options. The bar offers

a creative cocktail menu and serves quality local and regional brews. Closed Monday & Tuesday.

GW FINS
808 Bienville, New Orleans, 504-581-3467
www.GWFins.com
CUISINE: Seafood
DRINKS: Full Bar
SERVING: Dinner
PRICE RANGE: $$$
NEIGHBORHOOD: French Quarter
Here you'll find the finest quality seafood from around the world. Menu favorites include: Whole roasted Red Snapper and Blue Nose Bass from New Zealand. Try the Lobster Dumplings served with Fennel and Tomatoes and you'll be back for more. If there's room for dessert, try the individual homemade apple pie served warm and topped with vanilla ice cream. Their wine list is very impressive with more than 100 labels, most available by the glass.

GUY'S PO-BOYS

5259 Magazine St, New Orleans, 504-891-5025
No Website
CUISINE: Sandwiches/Cajun/Creole
DRINKS: No Booze
SERVING: Lunch; closed Sun
PRICE RANGE: $
NEIGHBORHOOD: West Riverside
Great place for lunch or a quick dinner. It's best to call ahead to order. Specialty – Po-boys. There are only about 15 seats so most people take their food to go. Get the grilled shrimp po'boy.

HERBSAINT

701 St Charles Ave, New Orleans, 504-524-4114
www.herbsaint.com/
CUISINE: French
DRINKS: Full Bar
SERVING: Lunch & Dinner weekdays, Dinner Sat; closed Sun
PRICE RANGE: $$$
NEIGHBORHOOD: Warehouse District
Located in a great spot with outdoor seating, this eatery offers an upscale menu of French and American cuisine. Favorites include: Louisiana Shrimp with Rice, artichoke and Maitake and the Muscovy Duck Leg Confit, which comes with a Dirty Rice with delicious hints of citrus "gastrique." This dish has been on the menu forever, and I always get it. Delicious desserts like their Greek Yogurt Cheesecake with roasted peaches.

HIGH HAT CAFÉ
4500 Freret St, New Orleans, 504-754-1336
www.highhatcafe.com/
CUISINE: Southern
DRINKS: Full Bar
SERVING: Lunch, Dinner
PRICE RANGE: $$
NEIGHBORHOOD: Uptown
This casual neighborhood eatery offers a menu specializing in the classic food from the Mississippi Delta. Menu favorites include: Catfish (fried, of course—I don't think they could ever cook catfish any other way) and Smoked Roasted Chicken. The bar has a nice wine list and serves local draft beers and craft cocktails.

THE JOINT

701 Mazant St, New Orleans, 504-949-3232
www.alwayssmokin.com
CUISINE: BBQ/Southern
DRINKS: Full Bar
SERVING: Lunch & Dinner; closed Sunday
PRICE RANGE: $$
NEIGHBORHOOD: Bywater
A menu of real Western-style BBQ keeps this place
packed. Great selections of pulled pork, beef brisket
and chicken and ribs. If you've never tasted peanut
butter pie, then you're in for a treat. (This pie turns
my stomach but those who like it *rave* about the
version to be found here.)

K-PAUL'S LOUISIANA KITCHEN

416 Chartres St, New Orleans, 504-596-2530
www.kpauls.com
CUISINE: Cajun/Creole/Southern
DRINKS: Full bar
SERVING: Dinner, Lunch – Thurs –Sat; closed Sun

PRICE RANGE: $$$
NEIGHBORHOOD: French Quarter
Chef Paul Prudhomme's down-home spot with a
menu of upscale Cajun fare. Favorites: Cheese
Stuffed Pork Chop and Blackened Louisiana Drum.
Expect large portions and delicious cocktails.

KILLER POBOYS
Erin Rose Bar
811 Conti St, New Orleans, 504-252-6745
www.killerpoboys.com
CUISINE: Sandwiches
DRINKS: Full bar
SERVING: Lunch & Dinner; closed Tues
PRICE RANGE: $$
NEIGHBORHOOD: French Quarter
Located in the back of the Erin Rose bar, this little
spot sells a variety of po'boys. Favorite: Pork belly
Po'boy with lime slaw. It's a real standout.

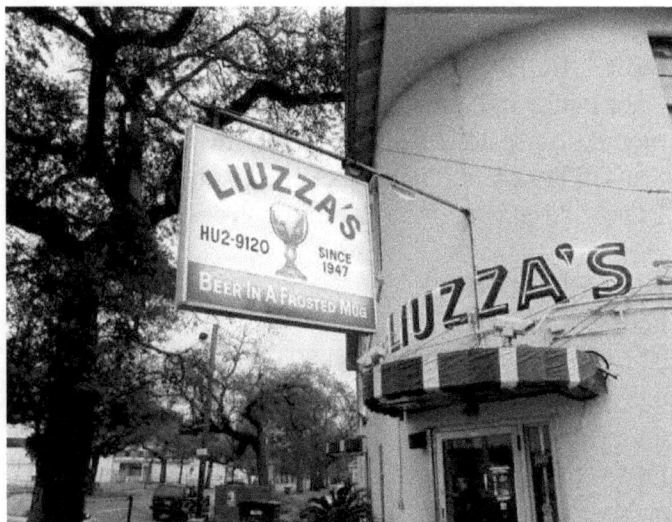

LIUZZA'S BY THE TRACK
1518 North Lopez, New Orleans, 504-218-7888
www.liuzzasnola.com
CUISINE: Cajun/Creole
DRINKS: Full Bar
SERVING: Lunch, Dinner
PRICE RANGE: $$
NEIGHBORHOOD: Mid-City
This eatery offers a New Orleans menu of Creole and
Cajun with a little Italian. Menu favorites include:
Shrimp, Corn & Okra Stew and Seafood Lasagna.
Their po' boys are so tasty but also too large to finish.
Closed Sundays.

LUCA EATS
7329 Cohn St, New Orleans, 504-866-1166
www.lucaeats.com
CUISINE: American (Traditional)

DRINKS: No Booze
SERVING: Breakfast & Lunch
PRICE RANGE: $$
NEIGHBORHOOD: Audubon
Popular café serving creative American fare. Menu
picks: Fried bell peppers & corn grits and Oreo
Beignets. Try their delicious homemade chips.

MAGASIN VIETNAMESE CAFÉ
4201 Magazine St, New Orleans, 504-896-7611
No Website
CUISINE: Vietnamese
DRINKS: No Booze
SERVING: Lunch, Dinner
PRICE RANGE: $$
NEIGHBORHOOD: East Riverside
This Vietnamese eater offers a variety of Pho. Menu
favorites include the Filet Mignon Pho (but I like the
Oxtail Pho better) and the Avocado Spring Roll. The
pig belly is braised for 40 hours until it forms a thick
sauce. A bare-bones eatery offering superior food.

MAHONY'S PO'BOYS & SEAFOOD
3454 Magazine St, New Orleans, 504-899-3374
www.mahonyspoboys.com
CUISINE: Cajun/Creole
DRINKS: Full Bar
SERVING: Lunch & Dinner
PRICE RANGE: $$$
NEIGHBORHOOD: East Riverside
This counter shop offers a great menu of sandwiches
and po'boys and it's hard to beat this place. Two
years in a row they won the Oak Street Po'boy

Festival (Po'boy Preservation Festival) with a po'boy that included fried chicken livers and Creole coleslaw. The Peacemaker po'boy has fried oysters, bacon and cheddar cheese. (Feel the heart attack coming on?) Great jambalaya also, as well as fried green tomatoes with remoulade sauce. It gets busy, so don't be surprised if there's a wait.

MANNING'S
519 Fulton St, New Orleans, 504-593-8118
www.caesars.com/harrahs-new-orleans/restaurants
CUISINE: American/Sports Bar
DRINKS: Full Bar
SERVING: Lunch, Dinner
PRICE RANGE: $$
NEIGHBORHOOD: Central Business District
Located at Harrah Casino, this Sports Bar offers a menu of American favorites with some Creole classics. This is the perfect place for sports fans with more than 30 flat screen TVs and a mega-screen TV.

MANNY RANDAZZO KING CAKES
3515 N Hullen St, Metairie, 504-456-1476

www.randazzokingcake.com/
CUISINE: Bakery
DRINKS: No Booze
SERVING: 6:30 a.m. – 5 p.m.
PRICE RANGE: $$
NEIGHBORHOOD: Metairie
Bakery specializing in king cakes in a variety of flavors. Specialty cakes baked and delivered year round.

MARJIE'S GRILL
320 S Broad Ave, New Orleans, 504-603-2234
www.marjiesgrill.com
CUISINE: Southern/Asian Fusion
DRINKS: Full bar
SERVING: Lunch & Dinner; closed Sun
PRICE RANGE: $$
NEIGHBORHOOD: Tulane / Gravier / Mid-City
Casual eatery specializing in Southern Asian cuisine mixed creatively together with Gulf ingredients. Try an order of pig knuckles—salty and crispy, covered with cane syrup. There's a BBQ pit out back where a lot of the food is coal-roasted. Shrimp are coated with cornmeal before frying. Favorites: BBQ pork shoulder and Spice-rubbed Gulf fish. Happy hour 4-6 weeknights.

MAYPOP
611 O'Keefe St, New Orleans, 504-518-6345
www.maypopnola.com
CUISINE: American (New)/Dim Sum
DRINKS: Full Bar

SERVING: Lunch, Dinner
PRICE RANGE: $$
NEIGHBORHOOD: Warehouse District
Popular eatery offers a menu of Southern-Asian
fusion mixed in with Creole specialties. Favorites:
House-cured meats and Red curry octopus pasta.
Menu changes regularly.

MEAUXBAR BISTRO
942 N Rampart St, New Orleans, 504-569-9979
www.meauxbar.com
CUISINE: French
DRINKS: Full Bar
SERVING: Dinner
PRICE RANGE: $$$
NEIGHBORHOOD: French Quarter
This sleek bistro offers a French menu of small and
large plates. The twist here is that they mix classic
French recipes using local ingredients and flavors
from Indochina. Favorites include: Louisiana Crab
and Peaches Salad and the Scallops & Pork Belly.
Great cocktails.

MERIL
424 Girod St, New Orleans, 504-526-3745
www.emerilsrestaurants.com/meril
CUISINE: American (New)
DRINKS: Full Bar
SERVING: Lunch, Dinner
PRICE RANGE: $$
NEIGHBORHOOD: Warehouse District
Great local eatery named after owner Emeril
Lagasse's daughter Meril is unlike his other spots in

the city, more modern (reclaimed wood in the interior) and adventurous and allows for numerous international influences. Favorites: Fried blue crab; Buttermilk biscuit with foie gras & blackberry jam; Spanish croquettes with ham, manchego, & piquillo pepper sauce; and Korean fried chicken. Creative desserts like Banana foster cake with ice cream or the lemon ice box pie. The cocktail menu is similarly adventurous, and ingredients are top-notch. Try the classic Hemingway daiquiri, as I did.

MIMI'S IN THE MARIGNY
2601 Royal St, New Orleans, 504-872-9868
www.mimismarigny.com
CUISINE: Tapas
DRINKS: Full Bar
SERVING: Dinner, Late night
PRICE RANGE: $$
NEIGHBORHOOD: Marigny

This great hipster dive serves a menu of tasty tapas. Menu favorites include: Goat Cheese Croquetas and Mushroom Manchego Toast. Live music.

MINT MODERN BISTRO & BAR
5100 Freret St, New Orleans, 504-218-5534
www.mintmodernbistro.com
WEBSITE DOWN AT PRESSTIME
CUISINE: Vietnamese
DRINKS: Full Bar
SERVING: Lunch & Dinner; closed Mon
PRICE RANGE: $$
NEIGHBORHOOD: Freret
A popular modern eatery offering up a menu of Vietnamese classics and other popular Asian dishes. Menu picks include: Vietnamese pork tacos and the Kim Chi Burger.

MOTHER'S RESTAURANT
401 Poydras St, New Orleans, 504-523-9656
www.mothersrestaurant.net/
CUISINE: Cajun/Creole, American (New), Soul Food, Southern
DRINKS: Beer & Wine Only
SERVING: Breakfast, Lunch & Dinner
PRICE RANGE: $$
NEIGHBORHOOD: Central Business District
This popular red-bricked cafeteria-style eatery has been dishing out Southern fare and delicious po' boys since the late 1930s. Menu favorites include all their sandwiches and the Fried chicken. On Saturday, they serve Dirty Rice *a la carte* or as a side with fried chicken. (Dirty rice gets its color and texture from the

hearts, gizzards and livers that are chopped or minced and then reduced in a skillet before being baked with long grain rice.)

N7

1117 Montegut St, New Orleans, No phone
www.n7nola.com
CUISINE: French; some Japanese influences
DRINKS: Full bar
SERVING: Dinner; closed Sun
PRICE RANGE: $$
NEIGHBORHOOD: St. Claude / Bywater
Casual French restaurant, with the emphasis on casual. There's an old red Citroen out front in the lush garden, just to give you a reminder that we're "going French" tonight. You go in and sit at the copper-topped bar. The antiques were collected by the owners over the years. The focus is on seafood and small plates, including "can to table" items, as they have lots of fancy tinned foods—lobster rillettes from France, calamari in spicy ragout from Portugal. You get the can, a crisp baguette, put it together with some wine and you've got a fine little meal. Favorites: Sake cured salmon and Escargot tempura. Nice wine list. Courtyard dining available.

NAPOLEON HOUSE
500 Chartres St, New Orleans, 504-524-9752
www.napoleonhouse.com
CUISINE: American/Cafe
DRINKS: Full Bar
SERVING: Lunch, Dinner
PRICE RANGE: $$
NEIGHBORHOOD: French Quarter
This French Quarter historic landmark offers a
Creole-Med menu with favorites like Muffalettas and
Po' Boys. Now, you can get Muffuletta in any
number of places in New Orleans, but it always made
sense to me to eat it in a classic building that's over
200 years old. Adds a lot of atmosphere. You know
what Muffaletta is, right? (It's ham, salami, pastrami,
provolone and Swiss cheeses piled high on a round
chewy loaf and topped with olive salad. What makes
it special is that it's heated, not served cold.) If you're
a fan of gin (as I am), try the classic Pimm's Cup; it's
refreshing and rarely served in other places.

NOLA PO'BOYS
908 Bourbon St, New Orleans, 504-522-2639
No Website
CUISINE: Seafood/Cajun/Creole
DRINKS: No Booze
SERVING: Lunch & Dinner
PRICE RANGE: $$
NEIGHBORHOOD: French Quarter
As the name states, this place sells Po'Boys and that's it. Great varieties like Fried catfish and Shrimp. Large portions.

PARASOL'S
2533 Constance St, New Orleans, 504-302-1543
No Website
CUISINE: Cajun/Creole/American

DRINKS: Full bar
SERVING: Lunch & Dinner
PRICE RANGE: $
NEIGHBORHOOD: Irish Channel
Popular among locals but the lucky tourists find their way here for the great sandwiches. You can get a half-and-half (two different sandwiches in one). Try the shrimp and catfish or the grilled chicken with fries. Note: there's a separate entrance is you're just coming to eat.

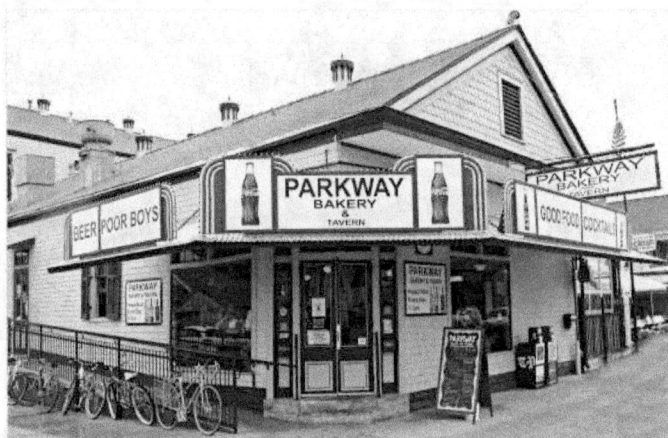

PARKWAY BAKERY AND TAVERN
538 Hagan Ave, New Orleans, 504-482-3047
www.parkwaypoorboys.com
CUISINE: Seafood/Sandwiches
DRINKS: Full Bar
SERVING: Lunch & Dinner; closed Tues
PRICE RANGE: $$$
NEIGHBORHOOD: Bayou St. John

Popular neighborhood haunt known for its classic po'boys, and though they go back as far as 1911, they didn't start serving po'boys till 1929. Katrina put the place under 6 feet of water, but it wasn't long before they reopened and were serving their signature hot roast beef po'boys. Other super po'boys are created from alligator sausage links, BBQ beef or the hot dog po'boy. There's a surf n turf po'boy which has fried shrimp mixed with the roast beef and smothered in gravy. Sounds scary, huh? Order carefully because one sandwich is good for two. The bar attracts a lively local crowd, and it's always fun here. (And you cat eat there, thus avoiding the lines.)

PASCAL'S MANALE
1838 Napoleon Ave, New Orleans, 504-895-4877
www.pascalsmanale.com
CUISINE: Cajun/Creole
DRINKS: Full Bar

SERVING: Lunch, Dinner daily except Sunday when it's closed.
PRICE RANGE: $$$
NEIGHBORHOOD: Milan
The better oyster bars in New Orleans get their oysters from their own beds. This place is one example of that practice. This family owned eatery offers a menu of classic Cajun and Creole cuisine. Menu favorites include their Original BBQ Shrimp. Reservations recommended.

PECHE SEAFOOD GRILL
800 Magazine St, New Orleans, 504-522-1744
www.pecherestaurant.com
CUISINE: Seafood
DRINKS: Full Bar
SERVING: Lunch, Dinner
PRICE RANGE: $$$
NEIGHBORHOOD: Warehouse District

Here you'll find a menu of coastal seafood made with a modern twist to old world cooking. Many of the dishes are prepared on an open hearth over hardwood coals. Menu favorites include: Grab meat and fresh oysters. If you can tear yourself away from the lovely raw bar selections, go for the Gulf wahoo prepared 3 ways: the head that comes with salsa verde; the belly, served with a soy & chili glaze; and the collar, offered with a tart pepper jelly. I've never seen a dish like this elsewhere. The owners here wanted to veer away from the typical fried seafood joints that proliferate in New Orleans. Maybe that's why the James Beard Foundation named it one of the Best New Restaurants in 2014.

PIZZA DELICIOUS
617 Piety St, New Orleans, 504-676-8482
www.pizzadelicious.com
CUISINE: Pizza/Italian
DRINKS: Beer & Wine Only
SERVING: Lunch & Dinner, closed Monday
PRICE RANGE: $$
NEIGHBORHOOD: Bywater
Casual counter-serve eatery serving thin-crust pizza. Small menu but usually crowded.

PYTHIAN MARKET
234 Loyola Ave, New Orleans, 504-481-9599
www.pythianmarket.com
CUISINE: Food Court
DRINKS: Full Bar
SERVING: 8 a.m. – 9 p.m.
PRICE RANGE: $$

NEIGHBORHOOD: Central Business District
In what was once the heart & soul of the African-American community, in 2018 the former Pythian "social club" was reimagined as a popular food court with eateries that emphasis local traditions. There's a pleasingly wide variety of choices, including everything from Brick-oven pizza, banh mi to Lobster Ceviche. Something for everyone.

R&O'S
216 Metairie-Hammond Hwy, Metairie, 504-831-1248
www.r-opizza.com
CUISINE: Pizza/Cajun/Creole
DRINKS: Full Bar
SERVING: Lunch daily, Dinner Wed - Sat
PRICE RANGE: $$
NEIGHBORHOOD: Metairie
A family restaurant that's usually packed and, trust me, it's because of the food, not the ambiance. Favorites include: hand tossed pizzas, Italian and seafood dishes, po'boys and their famous seafood gumbo. Still, if you only have time to visit this place once, get the roast beef po'boy. The beef is so tender. The gravy is rich and dark. The po'boy bread is toasted and the combination of these simple elements is wonderful. This place is a bit noisy and the TV is on for those wanting to watch the game.

R'EVOLUTION
777 Bienville St, New Orleans, 504-553-2277
www.revolutionnola.com/
CUISINE: Cajun/Creole

DRINKS: Full Bar
SERVING: Lunch, Dinner
PRICE RANGE: $$$$
NEIGHBORHOOD: French Quarter
This beautiful and luxurious restaurant offers an impressive menu of modern variations of Louisiana fare. The dishes showcase gulf fish, game and chops, salami, potted meats and terrines and pastas. Menu

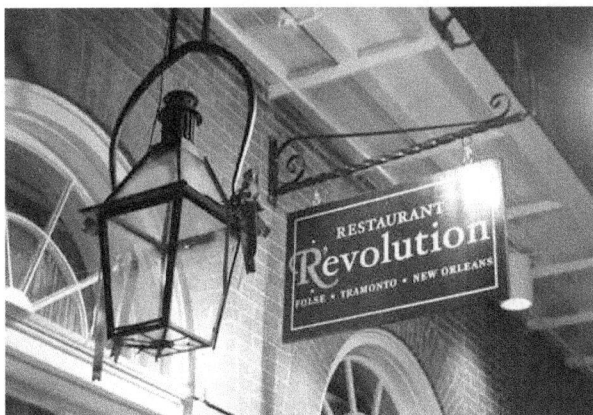

favorites include the Triptych of Quail with the birds Southern-fried and stuffed with boudin sausage. Known for their delicious sweetbreads and one of the most extensive wine lists in town.

RALPH'S ON THE PARK
900 City Park Ave, New Orleans, 504-488-1000
www.ralphsonthepark.com/
CUISINE: Cajun/Creole
DRINKS: Full Bar
SERVING: Lunch & Dinner, Dinner only on Tues & Sat.

PRICE RANGE: $$$
NEIGHBORHOOD: City Park
Located in an old 1860's house, this upscale eatery offers a classic dining experience. Menu favorites include: fried eggs with red eye gravy, whole Gulf fish, mouthwatering items like lamb ragout with

cream cheese grits or turtle soup with a liberal dash of sherry. Nice wine list. Popular Sunday brunch spot.

ROOK CAFÉ
4516 Freret St, New Orleans, 618-520-9843
No Website
CUISINE: Cafe
DRINKS: No Booze
SERVING: Breakfast, Lunch & Dinner
PRICE RANGE: $
NEIGHBORHOOD: Freret

Relaxed café ideal for hanging with friends or just bring a book or your laptop. Nice selection of coffees, lattes, espressos and muffins.

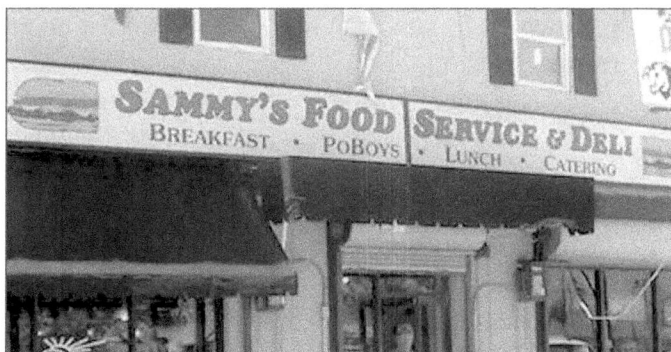

SAMMY'S
3000 Elysian Fields Ave, New Orleans, 504-947-0675
www.sammysfood.com
CUISINE: Peruvian
DRINKS: No Booze
SERVING: Breakfast, Lunch & Dinner; closed Sun
PRICE RANGE: $$
NEIGHBORHOOD: St. Roch
There's usually a line at the counter. Great Po'Boys and other favorites like Seafood eggplant. They have a great fried trout po'boy distinctive for its crispy cornmeal crust. Large portions. Poker machines.

SATSUMA CAFE
7901 Maple St, New Orleans, 504-309-5557
www.satsumacafe.com
CUISINE: Bakery/Cafe

DRINKS: No Booze
SERVING: Breakfast, Lunch
PRICE RANGE: $$
NEIGHBORHOOD: Uptown, Black Pearl
This is a bakery with a great menu of sandwiches, subs, gluten-free and vegan items. Here you'll find an interesting selection of fresh juices, like the tart and sweet Popeye juice. This is a very popular lunch spot that always crowded. Excellent coffee & cappuccino.

SEAWORTHY
630 Carondelet St, New Orleans, 504-930-3071
www.seaworthynola.com
CUISINE: Seafood
DRINKS: Full Bar
SERVING: Dinner, Lunch on Sat & Sun
PRICE RANGE: $$
NEIGHBORHOOD: Warehouse District
Small eatery offering locally sourced oysters and seafood. The oysters come with a choice of caviar, whether it's sturgeon, trout roe or bowfin—my advice is to try them all. Favorites: Grand Isle oysters and Popcorn shrimp. Happy hour specials. Tasty desserts.

SHAYA
4213 Magazine St, New Orleans, 504-891-4213
www.shayarestaurant.com
CUISINE: Middle Eastern/Mediterranean
DRINKS: Full bar
SERVING: Lunch & Dinner
PRICE RANGE: $$
NEIGHBORHOOD: Touro

Casual restaurant offering a menu of modern Israeli fare. The pita bread that comes from the oven is soft as a baby's pillow and the smell fills the room with a comforting aroma. Favorites: Crispy Halloumi (Peaches, Smoked Turkish Chilies, and Pecans) and Lamb Shank. Back patio.

SOBOU
310 Chartres Street, New Orleans, 504-552-4095
www.sobounola.com
CUISINE: Cajun/Creole
DRINKS: Full Bar
SERVING: Breakfast, Lunch, Dinner
PRICE RANGE: $$
NEIGHBORHOOD: French Quarter
Sobou offers a menu of comfort food with a modern twist. Menu favorites include: Crispy Oyster Taco and Crispy Chicken on the Bone. For a treat, try the

Foie Gras Float or the Cherries Jubilee & White Chocolate Bread Pudding.

ST. JAMES CHEESE CO.
5004 Prytania St, New Orleans, 504-899-4737
www.stjamescheese.com
CUISINE: Cheese Shop / Sandwiches
DRINKS: Beer & Wine Only
SERVING: Lunch & Dinner
PRICE RANGE: $$
NEIGHBORHOOD: Uptown
This tiny combination sandwich shop and market offers a great selection of cheeses. The charcuterie boards are among the best in town. The crowd is trendy and fun. In good weather, try to get a seat under the shade trees in the courtyard.

SYLVAIN
625 Chartres St, New Orleans, 504-265-8123
www.sylvainnola.com
CUISINE: American/Gastropub
DRINKS: Full Bar
SERVING: Dinner
PRICE RANGE: $$
NEIGHBORHOOD: French Quarter
This small gastropub offers an inventive menu with a strong bar serving delicious creative cocktails, like the Gunshop Fizz, made with rum and ginger beer they make here on the premises. A favorite of hipsters and foodies (and hip younger locals, who normally don't go into the French Quarter), it's also offers a nice courtyard for dining. Chef Alex Harrell offers up menu favorites like Braised Beef Cheeks, Prochetta

Po'Boys and Roasted Texas Quail as well as excellent daily specials.

TABLEAU
616 St Peter St, New Orleans, 504-934-3463
www.tableaufrenchquarter.com
CUISINE: Cajun/Creole
DRINKS: Full Bar
SERVING: Lunch, Dinner
PRICE RANGE: $$$
NEIGHBORHOOD: French Quarter
Located on Jackson Square at Le Petit Theatre, this is Dickie Brennan's newest restaurant. Chef Ben Thibodeaus offers a menu showcasing regional ingredients and classic French Creole cuisine. Menu favorites include Fried Eggplant Batons and Filet of Beef Bearnaise. There's an open kitchen in the main dining room so the guests can see the chef at work. This is a three-story restaurant with several private

dining rooms and courtyard seating. Open daily with brunch served on the weekends.

TOUPS MEATERY
845 N Carrollton Ave, New Orleans, 504-252-4999
www.toupsmeatery.com
CUISINE: Cajun/Creole
DRINKS: Full Bar
SERVING: Lunch, Dinner
PRICE RANGE: $$
NEIGHBORHOOD: Mid-City
Chef Isaac Toups offers a contemporary Cajun menu inspired by deep-rooted Louisiana family traditions. Here the food is excellent with menu favorites like: Pork Chops and Short Ribs. Dessert lovers should save room for the Doberge cake, a multi-layered sugary confection available in several flavors.

TURKEY AND THE WOLF
739 Jackson Ave, New Orleans, 504-218-7428
www.turkeyandthewolf.com
CUISINE: Sandwiches/Desserts
DRINKS: Full bar
SERVING: Lunch & Dinner; closed Tues
PRICE RANGE: $$
NEIGHBORHOOD: Lower Garden District
Funky no-frills sandwich shop with retro tables from the 1950s, weird salt shakers, etc. Menu features an inventive list of sandwiches and cocktails. Favorites: Chicken pot pie and Lamb neck roti (with cucumber and onions). The chef here is gourmet-trained, but likes things on the casual side. Very high quality food is served here.

VERTI MARTE
1201 Royal St, New Orleans, 504-525-4767
No Website
CUISINE: Sandwiches/Salad
DRINKS: Beer & Wine
SERVING: Open 24 hours
PRICE RANGE: $
NEIGHBORHOOD: French Quarter

Market and deli known for decades for its Creole inspired sandwiches. Popular stop for those out drinking all night. Favorite: Jazz po'boy made with a heaping pile of roast turkey, ham, American and Swiss cheese, sautéed mushrooms, tomatoes, Cajun seasoned grilled shrimp and their "special" sauce. The muffuletta here (served hot or cold) has more meat than beard, which is really good.

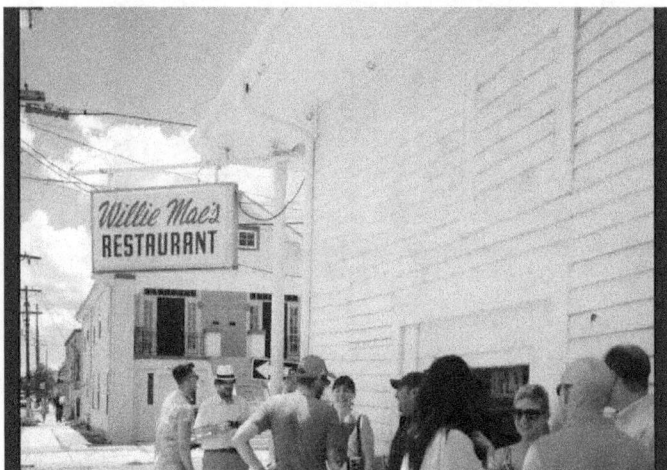

WILLIE MAE'S SCOTCH HOUSE
2401 St Ann St, New Orleans, 504-822-9503
www.williemaesnola.com/
CUISINE: Southern, Comfort Food
DRINKS: No Booze
SERVING: Breakfast, Lunch
PRICE RANGE: $$
NEIGHBORHOOD: Mid-City, Treme

Willie Mae's is known for its delicious comfort food like their America's Best Fried Chicken. The only drawback is that it's a bit out of the way. Closed Sundays.

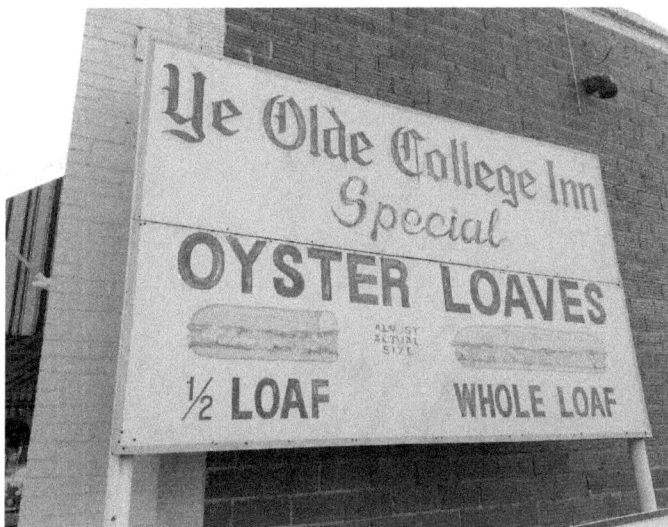

YE OLDE COLLEGE INN
3000 S Carrollton Ave, New Orleans, 504-866-3683
www.collegeinn1933.com
CUISINE: Southern/Creole/Cajun/American
DRINKS: Full bar
SERVING: Dinner; closed Sun & Mon
PRICE RANGE: $$
NEIGHBORHOOD: Gert Town
Casual eatery with a nice menu of Southern-Creole comfort food. Favorites Crawfish and Seafood gumbo. You must try their fried bread pudding for dessert.

NIGHTLIFE

WWOZ 90.7 FM
www.wwoz.org
Tune in to this radio station when you first get to town. It plays a lot of jazz & blues, but it's completely dedicated to the local music scene. A good way to find out what's going on. This will certainly get you in the right mood to party in New Orleans.

BAR TONIQUE
820 N Rampart St, New Orleans, 504-324-6045
www.bartonique.com
Popular among locals and visitors, this neighborhood bar mixes up classic cocktails with fresh ingredients. Great place to stop for a cocktail before dinner.

BJ'S LOUNGE
4301 Burgundy St, New Orleans, 504-945-9256
No Website
NEIGHBORHOOD: Bywater
If you like crowded smoke filled dive bars, this is
your place. It's usually packed with locals who know
each other. There's live music on Monday nights
featuring bands like King James and the Special Men.
Free red beans & rice on Mondays. Pool tables. Cash
only.

BUD RIP'S
900 Piety St, New Orleans, 504-945-5762
No Website
NEIGHBORHOOD: Bywater
This is just a classic neighborhood bar with TVs
being the only frills. Some call it a dive bar, but they
still show up for happy hour. There is also a pool
table, dartboard and video poker. Smoking allowed.

CANDLELIGHT LOUNGE
925 North Robertson St, New Orleans, 504-525-4748
No Website
NEIGHBORHOOD: Treme
This popular Jazz & Blues Club happens to be a
favorite stop for the secodline parades and the Treme
Brass Band makes a stop here every Wednesday night
and takes the stage. Cheap drinks and very friendly
crowd. Cover on Wednesday nights.

CAROUSEL PIANO BAR & LOUNGE
Hotel Monteleone
214 Rue Royal, New Orleans, 504-523-3341
www.hotelmonteleone.com/new-orleans-dining-entertainment/carousel-bar-lounge/
NEIGHBORHOOD: French Quarter
Here you can enjoy live jazz, blues, a mint julep, and people watch without moving as it's the only revolving bar in New Orleans. Located in the **Hotel Monteleone** overlooking Royal Street. This is a long-time favorite of locals and tourists who love to sit at the 24-seat revolving carousel bar. They've expanded the place so now there's a split-level viewing area as well as street level views.

CURE

4905 Freret St, New Orleans, 504-302-2357
www.curenola.com
NEIGHBORHOOD: Freret, Uptown
This is an unpretentious (although very hip) cocktail bar located in a repurposed firehouse on a dark corner that offers a creative menu of bar snacks. Not just a place to drink, but also a place to relax and enjoy the experience. Great selection of cocktails that have been designed by serious mixologists with a strong emphasis on the house-made bitters. The cocktail menu changes 8 times a year. Bar menu features items like Steak Tartare, Jamaican meat pies, baked crabcakes and Maitake Mushrooms. This was probably New Orleans's first craft cocktail bar, but there are numerous others ones now.

D.B.A.
618 Frenchman, New Orleans, 504-942-3731
www.dbaneworleans.com
NEIGHBORHOOD: Marigny
This live music club offers a roster of local and regional acts. The bar serves beer, wine and spirits in a smoke-free environment. Cover charge.

FRENCH 75 BAR

813 Bienville St, New Orleans, 504-523-5433
www.arnaudsrestaurant.com/french-75
NEIGHBORHOOD: French Quarter
This is a very popular New Orleans bar but it also
gets pretty smoky. The drinks are top notch and the
crowd is interesting as this is a side bar to Arnaud's,
one of the great dining spots of the French Quarter.
Try their Herbsaint Frappe, which might be called the
mojito for New Orleans, but flavored with anise
liqueur.

HI-HO LOUNGE

2239 St Claude Ave, 504-945-4446
No Website
NEIGHBORHOOD: St Roch
WEBSITE DOWN AT PRESSTIME
This neighborhood bar is also a live music venue that
has been one of the pioneers in the underground

alternative music scene. The variety of music includes indie rock, hip hop, electronic, jazz, funk and jam music. Other entertainment offered includes burlesque performances, comedy acts, and film screenings. No smoking allowed. Daily food specials offered and a guy cooks BBQ out front.

JEAN LAFITTE'S OLD ABSINTHE HOUSE
240 Bourbon St, New Orleans, 504-523-3181
https://www.ruebourbon.com/
 NEIGHBORHOOD: French Quarter
Built in 1807 as a corner grocery, this landmark saloon has become a must-see destination for locals and tourists. Unique round bar seating. Large cocktail

selection. No food but they have free popcorn and an inexpensive juke box.

LATITUDE 29
BIENVILLE HOUSE
321 N Peters St, New Orleans, 504-609-3811
www.latitude29nola.com
NEIGHBORHOOD: French Quarter
A Tiki-style gastropub with a great bar menu of exotic cocktails located in the Bienville House which dates back to the 1830s. Locals' hangout. There's a lovely courtyard with a pool. A place to get away from the noise and mayhem one usually finds in the French Quarter. Ask about the great cocktails not on the menu.

LOA
221 Camp St, New Orleans, 504-553-9550
www.ihhotel.com
Located in: International House
Popular New Orleans watering hole frequented by local artists, business owners and tourists. Located in the International House Hotel, this bar serves up a great selection of handcrafted cocktails, classics, and made to order concoctions.

MAPLE LEAF BAR
8316 Oak St, New Orleans, 504-866-9359
www.mapleleafbar.com
NEIGHBORHOOD: Uptown
This is dive live music venue is one of the longest operating music clubs in New Orleans. Live music 7 nights a week and they feature every music genre including blues, funk, R&B, rock, zydeco, jazz and

jam bands with a schedule that includes local performers and touring national acts.

MARKEY'S BAR
640 Louisa St, New Orleans, 504-943-0785
www.markeysbar.com
NEIGHBORHOOD: Bywater
This friendly neighborhood bar specializes in beer on tap and good bar food. This is a local hangout for watching the game serving up about 15 beers on tap. There are 8 TVs that play a variety of sports games.

MIMI'S IN THE MARIGNY
2601 Royal St, New Orleans, 504-872-9868
www.mimismarigny.com
NEIGHBORHOOD: Marigny
The DJ here plays a lot of old New Orleans "swamp music." There's a soul funk dance party on Saturday night.

OAK
8118 Oak St, New Orleans, 504-302-1485
www.oaknola.com
NEIGHBORHOOD: Uptown
This place offers an impressive selection of wines with nearly a hundred hand-selected bottles. The bartenders serve some great signature cocktails. Live music consists of jazz, acoustic folk or R&B. Full menu available.

PIRATE'S ALLEY
622 Pirates Alley, New Orleans, 504-524-9332
www.piratesalleycafe.com

NEIGHBORHOOD: French Quarter
Cozy little bar that opens very early (for those that need a rum before 10 a.m.) Serving great cocktails including Absinthe, served the traditional way with the absinthe water fountain, sugar cube and slotted spoon. Cash only.

ROCK 'N' BOWL
3016 S Carrollton Ave, New Orleans, 504-861-1700
www.rocknbowl.com
CUISINE: Bowling
DRINKS: Full bar
SERVING: Lunch & Dinner; closed Sun
PRICE RANGE: $$$
NEIGHBORHOOD: Gert Town
Bowling alley, bar, and stage for live music. Great selection of music. Menu is typical bar grub.

SAINTS & SINNERS
627 Bourbon St, New Orleans, 504-528-9307
http://saintsandsinnersnola.com
NEIGHBORHOOD: French Quarter
Channing Tatum's trendy two-level lounge with an old-time bordello feel. Don't expect to see Mr. Channing, even though it's usually filled with ladies hoping he'll make an appearance. Live DJ. Nice bar grub menu featuring favorites like Alligator tacos and gumbo fries.

SNAKE AND JAKE'S CHRISTMAS CLUB LOUNGE
7612 Oak St, New Orleans, 504-861-2802
www.snakeandjakes.com

NEIGHBORHOOD: Uptown
This is a small, neighborhood bar that great for late nights. It's been voted "New Orleans Best Dive Bar" many times and has a loyal following. Music provide by the jukebox. Smoking allowed.

SPOTTED CAT MUSIC CLUB
623 Frenchman, New Orleans, 504-943-3887
www.spottedcatmusicclub.com
NEIGHBORHOOD: Marigny
This live jazz bar is a favorite among the locals. The performers often ask people onstage to dance but there's also a small dance floor.

ST. ROCH TAVERN
1200 St Roch Ave, New Orleans, 504-945-0194

No Website
NEIGHBORHOOD: St Roch
This popular dive has a welcoming neighborhood feel with cheap drinks and a tasty bar menu. On Saturday nights there's a punk rock dance party that's become legendary. It's been called the sweatiest sissy bounce party in town. Cash only.

THE SWAMP
516 Bourbon St, New Orleans, 504-231-8519
www.bourbon-swamp.com
NEIGHBORHOOD: French Quarter
Popular nightspot with a gator theme and neon lights that features a mechanical bull in the courtyard. Wrap-around balcony typical of New Orleans. Upstairs, downstairs and outdoor patio filled with a young, attractive crowd. Offers great deals like 3 for 1 beers. Try the Swamp Juice – a giant cocktail of questionable ingredients, but it packs a punch.

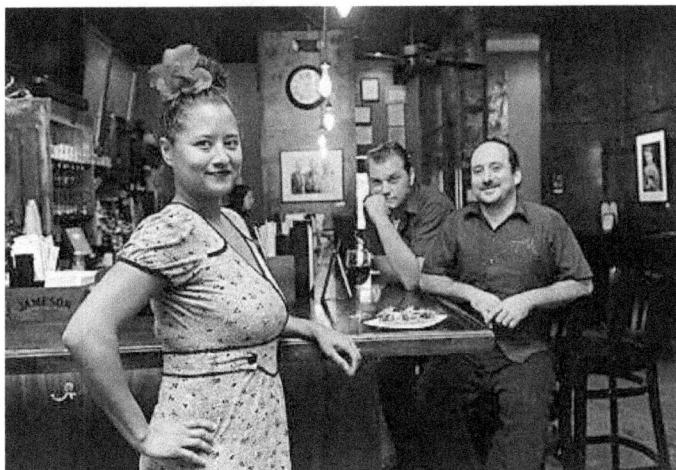

THREE MUSES

536 Frenchmen St, New Orleans, 504-252-4801
www.3musesnola.com/
NEIGHBORHOOD: Marigny
This relaxed nightspot offers a great mix of music and
cocktails. It's a locals' hangout and is usually
crowded. This is another haunt for those who like
specialty cocktails, like the Spaghetti Western
(bourbon, orange Campari & rosemary syrup). If you
want a table, be prepared to wait. Food available. No
smoking.

TRACEY'S

2604 Magazine St, New Orleans, 504-897-5413
www.traceysnola.com
NEIGHBORHOOD: Irish Channel

This Irish pub has perhaps the best roast beef po'boy in the city. But don't overlook the raw oysters and soft shell crabs. TVs, pool, and a menu of other po'boys.

TWELVE MILE LIMIT
500 S Telemachus St, New Orleans, 504-488-8114
www.twelvemilelimit.com
NEIGHBORHOOD: Mid-City
What other bar offers a haircut and a cocktail for $10 (Sundays only)? This unusual nightspot offers free food on Mondays and there's a live dating show on the last Thursday of the month. This dog-friendly bar features a pool table, craft cocktails, a menu heavily tilted toward BBQ and gourmet desserts (like the excellent doberge cake). The Great Idea cocktail is a mixture of vodka, amara and ginger beer. Smoking on the patio.

VITASCOPE HALL

601 Loyola Ave, New Orleans, 504-561-1234
www.neworleans.hyatt.com/en/hotel/dining/Vitascop
eHall.html
NEIGHBORHOOD: French Quarter
Named after the world's first for-profit movie theater
in New Orleans, this place features 42 flat screen TVs
and its own iPhone and Android application to keep
guests up to date. One of the best bars in New Orleans
with quite an active nightlife scene. Specialty
cocktails stand out here, like the Praline Sling, their
version of the Sazerac, made with bourbon, pecan
bitters, absinthe and caramel.

INDEX

www.ingramcontent.com/pod-product-compliance
Lightning Source LLC
La Vergne TN
LVHW021411080426
835508LV00020B/2551